CANINE INSTINCT

A Guide to Survival and Advancement in Corporate America

Ellen Burts-Cooper, PhD, MBA

authorHOUSE®

AuthorHouse™
1663 Liberty Drive
Bloomington, IN 47403
www.authorhouse.com
Phone: 1-800-839-8640

First published by AuthorHouse   6/30/2009

ISBN: 978-1-4389-3928-5 (sc)

Printed in the United States of America
Bloomington, Indiana

This book is printed on acid-free paper.

E-mail: improveconsulting@yahoo.com
improveconsulting.biz

This book is written for existing and aspiring managers looking to break into and beyond the midmanagement ranks in corporate America.

If you are truly looking to understand the dynamics at play when navigating the corporate game, I encourage you to read and practice the techniques in this guide. Hopefully, by understanding the views of the represented executive class, you can devise a strategy to join their ranks. It is equally important for current executives to understand the plight of the traditionally underrepresented and consider them as talent in the pipeline who are ready to lead major organizations.

For more information on the seminars and workshops that accompany this document, visit improveconsulting. biz

In memory of

G. R. Palmer and W. N. Bagby, pioneers in personal
development coaching

and

J. P. Burts, the greatest "executive" of them all

TABLE OF CONTENTS

PREFACE

Empowering individuals to exceed their potential, has been my focus for the last eleven years. This document is one example of information that I have compiled that has helped me in the corporate world, which I now use to benefit others. Through the work of my company, Improve Consulting and Training, I have stressed for individuals to take a proactive approach to self-development and continuous improvement. I work to help individuals exceed their potential by empowering them to go beyond what they think they are capable of achieving. I use a variety of techniques to teach participants to draw on their own energy as fuel for self-confidence and achievement.

Using multiple techniques helps create a sustainable model for achievement. This current document is just one of many unique approaches used to help others gain access to the networks that will afford them opportunities to compete equitably with their peers.

Individuals inherently want to do well but must be given an opportunity to gain access to resources and skills to fill developmental gaps. Even unintentionally, many new managers may be excluded from resources that are at the disposal of their colleagues, for a number of reasons. Through my work, I strive to empower others to gain equitable access to resources. *Most people, when given an opportunity to unleash their potential, find that what they are capable of achieving is frighteningly amazing.*

Through this document and beyond, my goal is to use what I have learned from the distinctive compilation of life and career events as an opportunity to coach and counsel others.

Instinct can be described as a natural or inherent aptitude. Canine instinct refers then to the complex and specific manner in which canines (both wild and domestic) react to environmental stimuli in ways that are essential for survival. Oftentimes, the intuition associated with instinctual responses cannot be learned; however, what can be learned are the traits and competencies associated with this behavior that lead members of the pack to the alpha leader position. When these qualities are incorporated into your style of leadership, they can be extremely beneficial for elevation into the leadership ranks. This guide breaks the natural instinct skills into manageable performance characteristics that can be studied and practiced, to develop optimal survival skills. More specifically, it explores some of the instinctual responses of canines, which are remarkably similar to the responses that have made leaders move past mere survival and thrive toward advancement in the corporate ranks.

Canine Instinct

A Guide to Survival and Advancement in Corporate America

Ellen Burts-Cooper, PhD, MBA
Improve Consulting and Training, LLC

Advancement
Thrive
Survival

ACKNOWLEDGMENTS

Humility, gratitude, and empathy are among the traits that I have worked consistently to cultivate. I am grateful for the many mentors, instructors, and professional coaches who have provided guidance and direction for me. I am humbled by their generosity, talent, and most importantly, their willingness to give back to others like myself. It is for these reasons that I make it my life's purpose and mission to assist others who may be able to benefit from my knowledge and experience.

Through interaction with individuals from varied economic, social, geographical, cultural, educational, and ethnic backgrounds, I have truly gained an appreciation for diverse working styles and a sincere compassion for the plight of others. I am thankful for these interactions, as they have broadened my perspective on a number of issues.

From a long list of both good and great managers, I have gained a wealth of experiences related to people management. From work in different types of businesses, I have had the opportunity to learn more about the application of business affairs under various industry conditions. Exposure to unique cross-functional opportunities throughout my career has led to tremendous personal and professional growth. I am appreciative of all my past mentor/coach interactions, since they have positively shaped my leadership style, and they continue to impact my personal and business interactions.

Most importantly, I am thankful for my family's continuous encouragement and for my partner in both life and business, Selwyn Cooper, for his unwavering support and patience through my many transitions.

Important Message to Readers

Techniques and tools will be introduced in this guide to help leaders become even greater leaders and advance in the corporate world. A leader must view himself or herself in two ways: (1) as a mentor and/or manager, using this as an opportunity to coach and (2) as a subordinate of his or her manager, using this relationship as an opportunity to learn. All techniques must be applied on both sides. Leaders must practice these skills and also impart them to their teams to be truly successful. So, all techniques should be studied and applied as a mentor and as a mentee. Engaged, equipped, and empowered leaders create engaged, equipped, and empowered teams. As a leader, you have to be proactive at identifying developmental opportunities for yourself and diligent about providing these opportunities for your team. After all, managers must work through their teams to accomplish their initiatives.

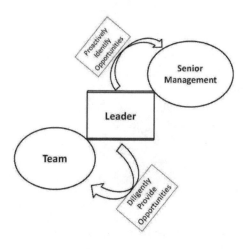

Prior to applying the concepts from this document, you should be able to complete the illustration above, by identifying activities that will allow you to make contributions in each of the surrounding boxes. Rather than thinking about just moving statically into one box at a time, you should consider making contributions simultaneously and advancing the entire structure to the next level.

CHAPTER 1

AN UNLIKELY
LEARNING SOURCE

L earning takes place through many avenues and takes on many diverse forms. The potential sources for learning are as varied as the learners. Don't be afraid to look to new types of resources to enrich your educational experience and add to your knowledge base.

After being in corporate America's mid to senior leadership ranks for ten years, I realized that a great deal of my success was due to navigating the landscape based on what I had learned from an unlikely source. I had gathered considerable knowledge from, get this, my canine obedience training certification program. The obedience in canine training is comparable to compliance in corporate learning. The foundation of canine obedience training is based on the principle of operant conditioning, or the understanding that a particular behavior that you choose to do has a particular consequence (positive or negative). This method of training can also be used in the workplace to teach accountability and ownership of actions.

Operant conditioning can have a positive or negative impact on the trainee. It is a scientific concept that is based on four principles: positive reinforcement, negative punishment, negative reinforcement, and positive punishment. Two of these principles are relevant for this guide: positive reinforcement and negative punishment. The other two involve the application of physical corrections for noncompliance, which are clearly not appropriate for corporate interactions. Simply put, positive reinforcement is shaping behavior by providing a reward (a treat for canines, which translates to increased compensation, an award, additional vacation, etc. for employees), whereas negative punishment is the removal of that reward (removing the toy or food bowl for canines, or taking away an office, giving a demotion, or reducing pay for employees).

Using reinforcements to increase the probability of a response occurring is critical with both canines and employees. Pavlov taught us that canines learn by association when there is a predictable relationship between two events. When applying this to modern-day training, there are two types of reinforcements: unconditioned (primary, highly desirable reinforcements that canines do not have to learn are rewarding, like treats) and conditioned (secondary reinforcements with no inherent meaning, which canines must learn to equate with the unconditioned reinforcer, like the word "good"). By learning that the conditioned reinforcer has a strong positive association with the unconditioned reinforcer, the word "good" and the treat become interchangeable. In other words, response to the first event happens in anticipation of the second. In the corporate world, this plays out through the association between performance evaluations and financial rewards, increased overall organizational performance and a rise in the stock price, a successful interview and a job offer, consistently exceeding objectives and promotion to a new level, high performance team coaching and positive survey rating, etc. Similar to canine interactions with their trainers, developing strong conditioned reinforcers increases communication and leads to happier, more energetic obedience or compliance between employees and their managers.

As a canine trainer, I learned about training styles and found that there are three dominant categories that trainers fall into, which mirror styles of corporate management. The compulsion trainers and managers have the "do it because I tell you" attitude, and the only motive for compliance is to avoid correction, rather than to display obedience out of respect. Positive-only trainers and managers provide rewards for compliance but rarely use any corrective techniques. The balanced trainer and manager use both positive methods and negative punishment (removing opportunity for the reward) to get results. Alpha leaders need to have balance and therefore have a variety of incentives for generating rewards and methods for building accountability.

So, yes, it's true. Although extensive functional knowledge was obtained from my bachelor's and doctorate in chemistry, my master's in business, several certifications, and from owning my own company, understanding the corporate game came from the most peculiar source. Or so I thought at the time. After years of practice, I noticed the similarities between techniques used by alpha canine leaders and by corporate executive leaders.

I initially attended the animal training certification course to volunteer my time with a nonprofit animal rescue organization. While learning the principles required for canine training, I started to see similarities in the workplace as a manager. I noted similarities between team members related to meeting and greeting, responding under duress, and performing while distractions are present (discussed in subsequent chapters). For management, the likeness was evident when providing rewards, developing training and development programs, and dealing with behavioral and performance issues.

Just as canines must have the proper socialization, humans must also learn how to react appropriately to new situations through exposure. Canines must be desensitized to common encounters. There is a requirement in the canine community for boundaries, limitations, and corrections. When exercised in moderation, these practices are not cruel but actually desired. Humans need these three sets of rules for order in their world as well. Legally and socially acceptable boundaries are established within every workplace and social setting. Limitations are established to ensure some sense of justice and to avoid discriminatory practices. When someone steps outside of a boundary or exceeds his or her limitations, a correction is applied. This is well known and tested in both worlds. This does not mean that individuality is lost; it means that everything is practiced in moderation.

This is why training and development are so critical in both worlds. In canine training, the various stages of learning are almost identical to those experienced by humans. In stage 1, or acquisition, learning happens through shaping and promoting consistency and reinforcement. In stage

2, or the automatic stage, learners (canine and human) give a specific behavior to a cue without being prompted. A cue in the animal world is a prompt or signal for action. It can be used interchangeably with an assigned action item or request in the corporate world. In the generalization stage, learners consistently demonstrate desired behaviors regardless of the location or trainer. In the final (maintenance) stage, learners consistently comply with cues in a variety of situations from 90 to 100 percent of the time.

Canine trainers are taught to manage situations and set the canine up to succeed, just as workplace mangers are expected to do. Canine trainers must also teach that there are consequences to undesirable behavior, which equate to accountability in the corporate world. Consistency is another crucial factor in setting up a successful canine training program, just as it is in corporate employee development programs. Lastly, providing a clear understanding of the requested expectations is equally critical in either scenario.

After some time, I found myself unconsciously applying some of the concepts from the canine training to maneuver through workplace situations. I was surprised to realize that my understanding of the corporate game was increasing, but I didn't quite make the connection to my animal training certification work until I received the same feedback on my corporate performance as I did in my canine training class. Feedback from both my manager and my canine training instructor was that I "related well to diverse personalities and provided effective coaching." Since my canine certification program required proficiency training for individual and group canine classes, I started to provide not only one-on-one coaching sessions but group coaching at work as well. In the training ring and in the corporate meeting room, group coaching provided the necessary environment for learning by visual observation and repetition. It was then I realized that when faced with scenarios in various business settings, I was using the same terminology as I worked through options. For example, whether coaching an employee on a work assignment or a canine on a command, providing encouragement is essential in both cases. Offering an encouraging statement such as "good job" is critical for optimal performance on both current and future assignments or commands. Conversely, when dealing with a performance issue, I use the same techniques in the canine training ring that I do in the corporate workplace. I apply a correction for inappropriate behavior and ask for a repeat of the command or action, until the desired result is achieved. After this, a reward (unconditioned reinforcer), followed by saying "good job" (conditioned reinforcer), was given.

Just as I had set-up a training plan for my canine trainee, as a manager, I also had to establish training and development plans for my human team members. Making the transition between canine obedience training and human development training was straightforward. Both required problem solving skills and plans for behavior modifications. Activity training in the canine world involves training on a specific activity designed to show the abilities of the canine and handler, just as technical training is intended for the employee to demonstrate competency to the management.

Other terminology that is common in a canine obedience training program that has results consistent with behaviors in the workplace includes the following: using a carrot and stick to achieve certain results or to attempt to induce compliance; capturing or waiting for the canine to perform or offer the desired behavior on its own and rewarding the canine when he does so; using lures as a way of tempting the canine with something he values, in an effort to draw him into a new behavior; proving or testing the canine's knowledge of a behavior; reinforcement, which is anything that increases the probability that a behavior will repeat itself; reward, which is something that is given in return for good behavior and offered or given for some service; and shaping or modifying an existing behavior by rewarding any progress toward a desired goal.

After the shock wore off and the laughter stopped, I began to document my findings. I found that during the course of studying canine behavior, I was able to better understand and navigate corporate America. Intriguing.

This document contains my observations of the similarities between canine behavior and interactions in the workplace. It is a unique approach to gaining leverage and increasing credibility in the business world by escalating your position through the fine-tuning of your instincts. I have found that in learning more about canine behavior, I have started to understand how to successfully maneuver in the business workplace. I have repeatedly used these techniques with a great deal of success in different industries. I have found that my application of these concepts has been one of the primary success factors in leading successful teams. In the beginning, I found myself applying what I learned from my animal training class without recognizing from where these critical techniques were originating. I was just gaining a clearer understanding of corporate dynamics and gaining success without realizing where my newfound style of adaptation was rooted. As I applied the concepts, I noticed improvements in my understanding and dealings with my team, my peers, and my management. Many of the improvements were related to the way I coached, provided rewards, and developed learning plans for my team. I studied the animal training concept of positive reinforcement of alternate behaviors. For extremely inappropriate workplace behavior, the solution related to animal training was to provide every possible opportunity to learn that a new behavior is more rewarding than the previous behavior.

It wasn't until I explored the connections further that I validated my thoughts and made even more connections. At first, I was surprised by the connection, then a bit amused by similarities, and finally intrigued by the possibilities of how I could use this new information to coach others on career advancement. I began to document my findings and explore ways to expand my techniques based on these similarities. After numerous constructive interactions both internal and external to the workplace (board meetings, community group meetings, academia, etc.), I began to think that I was on to something. I never shared my discovery until now. This model is presented an alternative way to view an issue and should serve as a supplementary learning opportunity.

Key leadership elements that will be discussed throughout this document include establishing credibility through performance and diverse interaction, flexing style traits to meet each person at his or her individual level of need, exercising empathy to see a situation from another's point of view, and gaining access to resources through positive social engagement.

ESTABLISHED CONNECTIONS

Most people understand the concept of unwavering loyalty that canines exhibit toward their human own-ers. Many of us have thought that if humans showed this same devoted loyalty toward each other, we might be better off. But there are many other, perhaps less obvi-ous, concepts within the canine community that humans would benefit from understanding and imitating in their interactions. The fact that canine social structures and internal drives are similar to those of humans has helped us to understand their behavior. However, this model uses canine behavior to understand our behavior within a business setting. It puts behavior modeling on a tactical level, so that individuals can be more deliberate about career advancement.

In canines, behavior drives are the instincts that shape their behavior. Almost everything a canine does can be attributed to a specific behavior drive. Drives are usually innate but can be controlled through training. Good trainers, like effective managers, influence the natural drives to create preferred behaviors. These drives, as described by the Animal Behavior College training program, are the social drive, the food drive, and the prey drive. In the human world, the social drive is similar to the canine and refers to interactions with others. The food drive is analogous to tempting and satisfying rewards, such as financial compensation, promotions, and other workplace perks. The prey drive in human behavior is parallel to the effort used to track and outperform the competition. In humans, securing an alpha spot can also be related to the natural drive for leadership. This is an innate quality for which no business, leadership, or professional development resource can teach. However, as with canine instinct, other behaviors can be learned that will help either further strengthen the innate behaviors of effective leaders or help fill developmental gaps for inexperienced or rising leaders.

Although genes define the outer limits of how and what animals can learn, their environment and experiences shape their reactions and overall dispositions. This explains why positive interactions and training are so impactful in creating alpha leaders. The same is true for humans. Although training can help modify undesired behaviors, genetics will always be a factor in how successful a training program is for canines or humans.

Another significant factor impacting behavior in the training ring and the corporate arena is temperament, the individual's reaction to various situations. Reactions in canines are well known to include fear, curiosity, willingness, courage, aggression, etc. These are indistinguishable from human categories of reactions. By knowing this, managers can adjust their styles to deal with employees based on their manner of thinking, behaving, reacting, and other individual characteristics.

Some of the personality identification types of canines include the following:

- Timid, shy, and fearful
- Nervous, stressed, and restless
- Sedate and tranquil
- Responsible and eager
- Stubborn and dominant
- Hyperactive and excitable
- Aggressive and combative

Most readers of this document will be able to fit themselves into one of the categories listed above and can name at least one person who would fit into each of these categories. Just as trainers use these categories to customize a canine training plan, managers can use these same categories to help employees as well as themselves, to create customized development plans. Aspiring alpha leaders can also use this information to interact more positively with others in the workplace. Taking the time to understand the personality types of others provides a clear advantage for successfully navigating a diverse workplace through more engaging communication.

THE BID FOR POWER: CONTROLLING THE ALPHA POSITION

In the canine world, there needs to be order. Within the pack, there always exists an alpha member. This hierarchical design closely resembles employees and the executive rank. A certain amount of control is exercised by the alpha or dominant members of a pack. The "pack" is equivalent to the "team" in the corporate world. The alpha members have "earned" these positions of power, which are established through order and rank. Humans typically think that only when an alpha member moves on or gives up his or her rank, can another member move up. However, the hierarchy in a wild canine pack is fluid and will change if circumstances are altered. Based on this principle, there is hope for humans to command senior positions through fair play and performance. Knowing this, how do you manage as a member of the pack or elevate your way to the "alpha" position? Know that there is always more room for differentiated talent. The days of the long tenure are fading, and competition will require a continuous replacement of leaders. The top spots have to be continuously replenished with talent that can gain control of valuable resources; it is then that a bid for power can ensue.

CANINE BEHAVIOR AND CORPORATE INTERACTIONS

In the canine world, the rules are clear and instinctively known by the entire pack. This does not directly translate to the corporate world. Typically, the human resources (HR) department is responsible for setting the rules for engagement, and through HR guidelines, consistent practices are instituted in regard to human-to-human interaction. However, beyond this established control, there are unwritten "rules" that have been established as core parts of the corporate survival game. These rules are not documented but are certainly real—real ways to ascend the corporate ladder that are known traditionally and exclusively to a select few. Individuals outside of the "selected elite" might start to rise through the ranks but still do not comprise a critical mass in many areas. So, do you find a coach in the upper tier to teach you the game? Do you study numerous business books and figure out the game for yourself? Do you keep your head down, work hard, and trust that the ranks will be kind to you? Quite possibly, all of these ways can work. Or do you study a similar behavior among, in this case, canines, and uncover useful behavioral approaches and techniques? The former methodologies are geared toward understanding specific interactions in a particular organization; in contrast, the latter teaches a behavioral understanding that can be applied more broadly. The link to canine behavior and corporate workplace interactions, through rewards, consequences for noncompliance, and behavior modification is a relatively new approach that I have used to personally navigate the business environment. This technique applies to not only the workplace but also to critical networking interactions beyond the corporate environment that are vital to a comprehensive learning and growth experience. Much of what is learned outside the place of employment is directly applicable to career progression.

With many animals, specifically canines, there is also a strong need for consistency, discipline, and praise. This is really not different from the basic needs of humans. Consistency provides the framework from which we base our daily interactions. Discipline, although often resisted, is absolutely required to establish and maintain order. If humans comply with the rules, they often receive highly desired praise for their actions. Provide consistency in the way employees are asked to perform, respond with discipline, and reward with praise. For canines, the expectations to perform a command are clearly given in the same manner each time, and a positive reinforcer is given to reward the desired response or is removed for noncompliance. Simple. So why are corporate interactions so complex? Perhaps because there are numerous other elements needed to maintain the pack. These elements are also essential factors that establish order, provide leadership, and maintain control.

So, the various techniques for climbing the corporate ladder that have been learned thus far should still be used. This model does not negate them; it simply adds more meaning. It sheds additional light on the "why" through behavioral understanding and the "how" of social interactions. So, the canine-corporate behavior model is a supplemental tool for understanding and navigating interactions needed for career advancement.

Key Points—Chapter 1

- Find nontraditional ways to supplement your corporate learning experience.
- Leaders in the alpha position must offer praise, provide consistency, and apply discipline.
- For management, awareness of employee traits that resemble categories of canine traits is evident in the manner in which rewards, training, development, and performance issues are managed.
- The canine-corporate model explores some of the instinctual responses of canines, which are remarkably close to the same responses that have helped leaders advance through the corporate ranks.

CHAPTER 2

USING THE CANINE BE-HAVIORAL INTERACTION MODEL TO UNDERSTAND WORKPLACE BEHAVIOR

Strong leaders not only understand the model for success but also find unique ways to deliver to their organizations while maintaining uncompromising integrity. During the navigation of corporate America, becoming an exceptional leader will require consistent execution and a solid understanding of acceptable behavior and social interactions.

To plot a successful course, a map must be created from the behavioral understanding of canine-canine and canine-human relationships. Knowledge of the power-gain activities, exhibiting acceptable conduct, and taking the appropriate actions are fundamental. Just as in the wild canine world, the alpha leader maneuvers in such a way as to gain and retain power over the pack through the demonstration of certain behavioral traits, such as showing leadership, and providing protection for the pack. The alpha leader uses its instincts to determine what activities are critical to survival, such as finding food, water, and shelter. Then the alpha leader behaves as a guardian over the pack. Finally, the alpha leader performs the necessary tasks to keep the pack functioning and in order. This is accomplished through established routines (also true in the domestic canine world), endurance, and awareness, just as in the business world, where managers must go through these same three steps to create and maintain order on their teams:

- First, the critical activities must be prioritized.
- Second, the conduct required to perform these activities must be applied.
- Third, the appropriate actions required to reach a desired performance level must be understood.

PRIORITIZING CRITICAL ACTIVITIES

As a leader, the determination of critical activities, or those actions that are required for team survival, must be decided, and the leader's actions must validate the priorities. Oftentimes, the critical hard skill tasks are based on generating revenue, cutting costs, and satisfying customers' requirements. Execution of these tasks is typically heavily weighted on a performance appraisal in the human world. Meeting organizational objectives is paramount. However, there are other critical factors necessary for leading a pack or a team. These critical soft skill activities include developing themselves and their teams, setting clear and compelling visions, holding themselves and their teams accountable, and rewarding desirable behavior. In the canine community, a good pack leader does three additional tasks: looks after the pack by supplying the necessary resources for survival, keeps the pack aware of external threats, and remains uncompromising and tough with the pack when necessary. A thorough leader must also incorporate these three activities into his or her leadership approach. The leader must also determine how much to weigh the hard vs. the soft skills and must know the relevance of each, based on changing environments.

It is amazing that canines balance their version of hard skills (gathering food and water) with soft (nurturing of the pack) skills. Through this process, canine leaders typically have sufficient strength to earn respect rather than having to resort to constant bullying to retain control. Good leaders, whether canine or human, should not have to continuously remind the pack that they are in control. Once order is established, they maintain their status over their subordinates through strength and wisdom. Status is lost in both worlds when order and respect deteriorate. This happens through inconsistency in the leadership style, loss of task priority, inappropriate extension of boundaries, slippage in discipline around limitations, and absence of visible corrections.

APPLYING THE REQUIRED CONDUCT

When canines face challenges, their responses are based on four choices: flight, fight, avoidance, or submission. Humans, perhaps unknowingly, respond with these same four options. Without the proper preparation and forethought, humans may feel forced to quickly choose an option that may be inappropriate for the circumstances. Nonetheless, whatever the choice, it typically fits into one of these four categories.

Flight

What happens when you are faced with an encounter in the business world, and your fear of consequence leads to your flight or retreat from the issue? During the moment of the encounter, this usually seems like the easiest of the four options. Just leave the situation. The problem is that the situation will not necessarily go away. How do you tell when running away will save you from dealing with a substantial problem in the end? There may actually be times when "running away" is acceptable. When you are faced with a no-win situation, and the risk of failure is imminent, retreating is wise. However, you only get a few times to use this option before being seen as a coward. With this option, having the skill to quickly calculate risk vs. reward is necessary. Developing this skill can be achieved at lower risk through the lessons of present and past alpha leaders. Studying when this technique was applied by successful, visionary leaders can help create a decision guide for aspiring leaders. Leaders can either be interviewed for the information or, more realistically, there are profiles of extraordinary leaders that can be used to find this information. Another approach for acquiring this skill is to document various scenarios that are likely to occur in your particular business environment. Carefully think through the situations, and list the circumstances in which flight would be appropriate, along with the risks for each.

Fight

Fearful canines may find it difficult to read and/or send signals, which often leads to a combative interaction. They misread sniffing, the equivalent of the human handshake, and fight when they feel threatened or challenged. In human terms, this hostility is often displayed in a bad first interaction, which typically does not lead to a physical altercation but rather to a strained relationship. Between humans, a fight can occur when a more junior person challenges someone with more authority. The lower-ranked employee might then stand his or her ground on a point or make a stand on an issue and refuse to back down. Possessing good insight and knowing which battles to fight are absolutely crucial skills both when using this option and for a leader at any level. Unfortunately, experience is the best teacher. However, a good rule of thumb when faced with this decision is to quickly assess the situation and ask yourself, *If I win this battle, will the reward move me closer to the elevated leadership?* or conversely, *Will losing this battle move me further away from an alpha leader's role?* If you are able to answer yes to the first question and no to the second, then the fight option is probably appropriate. However, exercising this option too frequently can make a person appear to be confrontational and can threaten his or her credibility and render the person ineffective when an appropriate battle arises.

Avoidance

Avoiding a situation altogether can be the best choice if the risk of the encounter outweighs the benefit of confrontation. Being astute enough to anticipate a potentially negative situation and steer clear has its advantages. However, misreading a situation and potentially passing up an opportunity can be detrimental to career movement. The proper use of the avoidance technique requires the keen ability to predict outcomes and the ability to distinguish between unproductive challenges and potential opportunities. As with the fight option, experience is critical to making the right decision. In the meantime, listing the mistakes of other leaders and studying the actions that led to these can be useful. Typically, there are really no unique workplace issues; they are merely a replication of past events. By analyzing past mistakes and the resultant actions, a list can be developed that includes potential sources of risk. The list must be continuously updated and reviewed, so that when conditions arise that resemble those on this list, you will be familiar enough with them to recognize potential negativity. This technique is extremely useful in personal and social situations, as well. A miss here could cause a substantial setback. Extensive experience in reading various situations is a critical skill when evoking the avoidance option. Good business acumen gained through a range of experiences over time is the best predictor of success with this technique.

Submission

Is submission ever a wise option? Why, certainly. Submission is the most widely used of these techniques. Submission refers to obedience or compliance with the established norms. In the canine world, it can be viewed as giving in or giving up, by allowing the more alpha member to take control of the situation. However, in a broader sense, it can be simply viewed as following the rules. In what circumstances is compliance or obedience appropriate? Probably, in the majority of circumstances. Leaders typically assimilate to the normal business policies that help maintain order. However, over-assimilation can be viewed as the lack of creativity and as the inability to break away from the mediocrity of the pack. Establishing a distinction from the norm is valuable for leaders, to provide inspiration and vision. So, a critical skill needed when choosing this option is having a combination of courage and wisdom. Knowing the basic compliance and HR rules of your organization will help you to know when an incident is not negotiable and submission is absolutely required. it might be helpful to keep a personal inventory of what you will and won't stand for, either on a moral or ethical basis. The list of items could be summarized into three categories: must accept, absolutely will not accept, and might accept depending on certain factors that you can also list. Oftentimes, alpha leaders find it necessary to defy accepted norms or rules. Wisdom is needed to know when to step outside of the established practices. Wisdom is also needed to know when resistance to established procedures is culturally and socially acceptable and beneficial for career movement. Courage is needed to follow through with the decision to resist established practices.

SUMMARY AND EXAMPLES OF THE FOUR OPTIONS

So, when faced with an issue, do you take flight by running off, stay and fight, avoid the situation, or just submit to it? Knowing your skills and strengths is crucial to understanding which option to choose. If none are proactively chosen, then you inadvertently respond using one of the techniques without calculation and thought. The lack of forethought in the canine world can lead to grave circumstances. In the corporate world, reacting without consideration is viewed as reckless and uncharacteristic of effective alpha leaders. Careers are typically filled with a variety of selections from each of these techniques. So, choosing a technique certainly depends on the interaction, your strengths, and where you are in your career. Riskier moves that go bad can be tougher to overcome in later stages of a career. Although you have time to rebound from them when starting out, you may not have the credibility to recover in the more advanced phases of a career.

Setting realistic personal and team goals, establishing a compelling vision, and working toward this vision under varied environments help managers move to optimal performance levels. This is analogous to the canine world, where established routines, endurance, and awareness lead to these levels of performance.

Moving On to Avoid Character Loss—The Flight Option

When is it acceptable to flee from a situation or an obligation? Imagine that you are part of a high profile, non-profit board; you were recently appointed, in large part, as a result of the executive support you received from your organization. For the past five years, the board has been financially sound and has been consistently recognized for its commitment and work in the urban communities. As a result of recent economic conditions, the board's financial situation is bleak. The number of donors is steadily decreasing, along with the amount of their pledges. The organization is faced with closing its doors or changing its mission to be eligible for additional funding from a local political party. This funding would certainly keep the organization moving but would require you and the other board members to accept biased direction from the political group. You personally knew the founder of the nonprofit and are quite certain that his mission was to serve citizens in economically depressed areas. The new focus would allow for 10 percent of the workers' time to be dedicated to the original mission and 90 percent of the time (and most of the funding) to be directed toward a middle-class, suburban population who were strong supporters of candidates from this political party. You and several others strongly oppose the vote, but when the motion carries, you have to make a decision. You put up a fight but lose this battle. Even if you had chosen to try and avoid the situation by not voting, the problem would still remain. Now, your options are to submit or to choose the flight option and resign from the board. Integrity comes into play in this decision, and for truly remarkable leaders, this would be a situation where there is only one option—flight.

Earlier in this chapter, we discussed that there are situations when "running away" may be acceptable. This was in a clearly a no-win situation with the highest possible risk—risk of reputational damage. The loss of a position on a prominent corporate-appointed board is career-altering, but loss of integrity constitutes business and personal collapse. Failure was imminent, and therefore, retreating was wise. Rebuilding personal integrity is virtually impossible at any point in a career.

Picking Your Battle, Standing Your Ground—The Fight Option

Opportunities to use the fight technique surface quite often. Deciding which battles are worth fighting will serve any leader well. Examples demonstrating when to use this technique are plentiful at work, home, and in social settings. Differences in style and approach due to generation gaps and gender differences are both highly charged sources of issues leading to malicious battles. A typical example in the business environment is when an action item from management conflicts with an employee's belief system. Another occasion for fight-related issues arises when a viewpoint is ignored, and an employee believes that he or she must push to be heard. A fight situation also commonly occurs when organizational change is not managed for large initiatives, opening the floodgates for resistant behavior. The threat of new ideas is another likely source of internal feuds.

Suppose you are in a meeting where the objective is to decide on a new product design. You make the point that feedback should be gathered from the customer prior to making any prototypes. You believe that this is critical to developing a product that will meet customer requirements. You are dismissed by a peer who insists that he has a better way of accomplishing the task based on his substantially longer work history. Your peer wants to build the prototype first and believes that a good product will draw customers. What he has failed to realize is your extensive expertise in the matter being discussed. Based on your benchmark studies, you know that in your industry, 90 percent of customers prefer to provide input into the design of prototypes. Your data also shows that sales were less than 7 percent for products launched prior to customer input. In this meeting, you determine that it would not be appropriate to provide your background, which includes the fact that efficient new product commercialization was the topic of your doctorate dissertation and that you spent the first six years of your career successfully consulting with over twenty companies on the topic.

You find that you are losing control of the room and feel it is necessary to take charge of this discussion. You stand your ground, reiterate your case, and emphasize the need for support of your proposal. Your peer continues to escalate his voice to a point of awkward disagreement. You are aware of the method being forced by your peer and have seen it fail under numerous circumstances. Your peer is clearly basing his argument on incomplete data. At this point, you refuse to submit or take flight, because of the detrimental effect it will have on the team. You are too far into the situation for avoidance to be a reasonable option. You stay and fight. You still have one more decision—fight in the meeting in front of your team or take up the conversation later and engage one-on-one. Due to the seriousness of the issue, providing immediate clarity and resolution is more critical than the risk of appearing to be confrontational. You take on the fight, but you do so wisely, by providing data and facts to support your approach. You go to the white board and draw out the process map; you turn to your presentation and show statistically how the two arguments compare. You then offer to follow up with references from recent decisions made at similar companies who have taken comparable positions. After your peer backs down, you graciously acknowledge to your audience that the organization will be moving forward using your approach. You humbly let your peer know that you would certainly like his support to carry out the initiative. You have stood up for your strategy based on a solid fact-based line of reasoning and, most importantly, you modestly accepted the public win.

You have earned the respect from your peer, your management, and your team. It may take some time for your peer to come around to having lunch with you again, but you have his respect. It is usually not wise to fight, but when potential battles are encountered, knowing which one to fight is vital. Canine instinct allows you to quickly weigh the risks, benefits, and potential outcomes of a battle.

Preventing Unproductive Outcomes—The Avoidance Option

Having the prudence to think through a scenario and predict the profitability of the outcome is a core trait of a genuine alpha leader. Common ways to apply the avoidance method include steering clear of the following situations: involvement in inappropriate conversations, risky investments, unapproved activities, and unsolicited comments to the media.

When working with financial transactions, especially those having significant impact to external customers, knowing how to avoid pitfalls is a necessity. In corporate America, individuals are often faced with decisions involving forecasting customer demand to determine production levels. What if you were an IT manager with the task of advising the executive team on how much to invest in an upcoming technology release? The release should generate significant revenue, but it is obviously dependent on customer purchases. Economic challenges have made the market unstable, and you have limited information regarding customers' intent to purchase. You have a million discretionary dollars at your disposal but must make the case to the executive team to release the dollars.

If the technology sales are high, the investment will be considered justified based on the generated revenue and resulting profit. If you misjudge the customer demand, you might lose significant dollars during economically challenging times and risk being viewed as fiscally irresponsible—a fatal flaw among leaders. You are charged with the task, so flight is not an option. You agree with the technology release, so there is no need for a fight option. So, your choices are avoidance or submission. Submission is not really an option, since you are not being told to take a specific action; you have been given the authority to make the decision. So, how do you avoid the situation when it is present and visible? You don't. You avoid the activities that could result in a financially depleting decision. So, preparation is necessary to be more accurate in clearly predicting outcomes that avoid the hazards but not the opportunities.

Strategic avoidance is the required in this case. Unnecessary risk can be avoided by gathering customers' opinions up front to determine feasibility of the option. Additionally, calculating the marketing/business probability of success will help mitigate risk. So, in this case, you decide to invest a portion of the discretionary funding to solicit customer feedback and to gather and analyze market data. Once the risk vs. reward is measured and the analysis is complete, you can make a revised proposal that may substantially reduce the projected investment. A customized approach will lessen the potential monetary loss.

Giving In and Learning to Trust—The Submission Option

Let's review an example of acceptable submission to a situation. You have been assigned a task by your senior management, and you are not gaining support for this activity among your peers or the majority of the organization. You try reasoning with others but cannot seem to get on board a critical mass despite numerous logical attempts. The root of the issues resides in a difference in objectives. The organization has been behaving one way, and you are now asking them to accept a new initiative, which may fundamentally change the way they have been working for the last ten years. Knowing your struggle, your management still insists that you get this done and now has added a fast-approaching deadline. You later are told that there is information that you are not (and neither are others outside of the senior management ranks) privy to, which would reveal the importance of executing this activity in the best interests of the organization. Your management can't disclose the information but does tell you that inability to implement will result in catastrophic loss for the organization. You are strongly warned not to disclose even the small amount of information you know but to still get this done. Because of limited information, you really are unsure if this is really in the best interest of the organization, and you believe strongly that this is just another tactic of a new management regime to assert power by instituting a program that carries their innovative identity. You try one last attempt to persuade management to allow you to dig into the data and analyze the best approach for the organization but are told, for the third and last time, that this is not negotiable and just to get it done. Rather than schedule more individual meetings trying to persuade, influence, and convince, you call the organization together and provide the strategy and assign the operational tasks. You make it clear that this is a mandate from senior management. You don't really know if this move is truly in the best interest of the organization, but you choose to submit to the action you were assigned. When faced with a decision like this, you have to examine whether your past experiences have caused a lack of trust toward senior management, or to determine if you are carrying baggage that clouds your ability to trust your instinct telling you that something is not quite right.. Perhaps the management is working in your organization's best interest, so you would be a recipient of any good fortune resulting from deploying the initiative. More about the impact of past experiences on making current decisions will be discussed in Chapter 4.

Was there another option? Was submission the wise choice? Absolutely. Resistance or choosing the fight option would both have proved to be career-limiting (or potentially career-ending) moves.

Key Points—Chapter 2

- Response to issues is based on four choices: flight, fight, avoidance, or submission.
- Knowing your skills and strengths is crucial to understanding which option to choose.
- When you take flight, move on to avoid character loss.
- If you choose to fight, pick the right battle and stand your ground.
- Avoiding negative situations allows you to prevent unproductive outcomes.
- Submission requires that you give in and learn to trust.
- Prioritize critical activities, and know the appropriate actions to reach a desired performance level.

CHAPTER 3

REACHING DESIRED PER-
FORMANCE THROUGH
APPROPRIATE ACTION

In addition to proper social behavior and networking, leaders will have to perform under a wide range of conditions, changing external environments, and challenging internal circumstances. Understanding the priority of action is a critical skill in an alpha leader's tool kit. Knowing when, where, and how to apply knowledge and acquired proficiencies increases the chances of moving higher in the management ranks.

Canine trainers are taught that there are three critical Ds required for optimal and sustainable behavior. Trainers are taught that canines should be able to perform or respond to commands even when distractions, distance, and duration are introduced. Performance in the absence of disruption does not carry the same weight and doesn't lead to repeated performance. Being able to function when disturbances are present is critical because this scenario mirrors reality. Similarly, in the corporate world, executing a strategy when the entire team is onboard is quite different from having to build consensus during execution.

Running an operation when the equipment malfunctions certainly adds more stress than when everything is operable. Offering a product or service to a customer when there are multiple comparative competitive items being offered creates a much more challenging sales environment. Implementing a new technology system with a sudden budget reduction forces prioritization much more so than with unconstrained finances. Any type of these otherwise routine daily functions now becomes much more complex and requires far greater effort with external forces present.

Simple tools are introduced in the chapter that help manage and practice the three Ds. These three Ds, when mastered, contribute to an essential fourth D, discipline, which is needed in any profession. Working in isolation is certainly not common. So, the sooner leaders start preparing for these potential threats, the more likely that they will be able to successfully thrive under pressure. The most experienced executives are not always able to predict potential threats, but knowing how to respond when unanticipated issues arise is the next best alternative. Therefore, introducing distractions, distance, and duration is as critical to canine training as it is to leadership development.

DISTRACTIONS

Education provides an entry into the corporate world and is essential for understanding basic functional concepts. Beyond education, there are numerous ways to maneuver through the environment. One way is through performance. Performance is the minimal price for entry into the corporate game. However, networking through social interactions and image through personal positioning gets you beyond the average players and headed for the alpha positions. It is not enough to just know your material to compete for the upper positions. You must know your craft and understand how to perform beyond what the books taught when pressure is applied. It is easy to read a concept and regurgitate it back on an exam. The alpha leaders know how to combine these "book smarts" with experience and still perform under duress.

Most nonleader canines understand basic commands at home but seem to forget them in public settings. They have learned the commands but have not mastered them under diverse conditions. The speed of the marketplace, the pressure to outperform competition, and the intolerance for mistakes, combined with the impatience of management for results and revenue, lead to a pressure-filled environment. Similarly, in the animal world, other canines, new scents, noises, etc., all contribute to distractions that make obedience to commands and skill mastery more difficult. In the business world, the notion that there are limited spots at the top for talented contributors is certainly true. So, what is the best way to secure one of these spots? To increase the odds of gaining an alpha position, learn to perform your craft in various industries, under different management styles, and in the face of external market challenges.

A good exercise to stay mentally stimulated and prepared is to frequently list all of the potential distractions present both internally and externally that could divert your plan. Along with each distraction, the immediate response and recovery plan should be listed. Due to the large number of potential disturbances, the list should only contain the major issues, prioritized by relevance to the completion of your task. This list should be updated regularly, as internal and external conditions change.

Distraction Evaluation Tool

Distraction Evaluation Tool					
Potential Threat	Anticipated Response	Recovery Plan	Severity* (1, 3, 5)	Probability of Occurrence* (1, 3, 5)	Priority** (Severity x Occurrence)

*criteria must be defined for your organization; **rank highest to lowest

DISTANCE

When a canine is given a command on and then off leash, the results can be quite varied. Tell the average canine to sit while watching, and you get one result. Turn your back or walk out of the room, and well … all bets may be off. How close does your management need to be to your project in order for the results to meet expectations? When independence is given, does the degree of task performance decrease? Does more autonomy increase the likelihood of failure? The idea is that leaders can be given tasks and can perform them with minimal supervision. The outcome exceeds expectations whether management is around or not. Being known for solid performance and execution of critical tasks without the constant need for management input is a required alpha trait. Alternatively, as a leader, what happens when you have to be away from your team? Can your team carry out basic and even complex functions when you are not intimately involved? Have you prepared your team to perform in your absence, and have you prepared yourself to perform in your management's absence?

To be prepared for the distance factor, equip your team to function in your absence by providing a clear plan, the necessary resources to carry out the job, and the freedom to do that job as they see fit. As leaders, the emphasis should be on what needs to get done more than the how it gets done. This is certainly not to say that we should not hold our team to high standards for work operations. It simply means that individual contributors should be allowed to think independently and be encouraged to solve problems creatively. Leaders should hold their management and themselves to these same criteria.

Succession planning is a critical part preparing for the distance factor. Having a candidate on your team who could reasonably perform your job should be the goal of every manager. Confident leaders know that they are not working themselves out of a job but are preparing both themselves and a member of their team for advancement.

Succession planning requires you to watch and continuously provide feedback on your team's performance. Give your team opportunities to take parts of your role even when you are in the office. Conversely, asking your management for the criteria for moving into their roles and also proactively taking on activities (within reason) that can alleviate burden from your management allows them to see you in their roles. Care should be taken to ensure that you know your management's style so that they are not threatened by your behavior. This will require You to work to develop a solid relationship with them. If the management is not proactive about providing opportunities, you will have to be creative in taking this approach and realize that it may take time.

Within various businesses, a range of management styles can be employed, depending on the culture of the business, the nature of the task, the nature of the workforce, and the personality and skills of the leaders. Some of the most common styles include the following:

- Autocratic
- Paternalistic
- Democratic
- *Laissez-faire*

Autocratic or authoritarian managers keep the information and decision making to themselves. Employees are expected to perform their work exactly according to the objectives and tasks that are set. As you can imagine, communication flows in one direction—from the senior management to the subordinates.

The paternalistic leadership style is also dictatorial, but the decisions tend to be in the best interests of the employees rather than the business. Within this style, the leader explains most of the decisions to the employees and ensures that their social and leisure needs are always met. Although communication is again generally downward, there is allowance for feedback to the senior management if it is needed to maintain employee happiness.

In the democratic management style, the senior management invites employees to take part in decision–making, and the outcomes are a result of agreement by the majority. Communication is abundant, and it extends in both directions.

The *laissez-faire* leadership style is one where the leader's role is peripheral or hands-off, and essentially, employees are allowed to manage their own areas of the business. Although the communication flow occurs in both directions, there is far less communication in comparison with other styles.

You must examine the various leadership styles to determine where your senior management most closely fits. If you determine that your manager fits in the democratic style, there is an obvious open door for you to have the succession planning conversation. Conversely, if your manager falls in the autocratic category for leadership, approaching him or her for any discussion comes with great risk. With the paternalistic leaders, you can discuss any issue, but you will need to show how this clearly satisfies a moral and/or social need. If your management falls in the laissez-faire category, there is enough communication flowing that opportunities for discussion exist, but the issues may need to be presented with strong evidence that it is a priority.

Most managers operate using a range of these styles; however, there is usually a dominant style that tends to surface more frequently and especially in stressful times. In addition to knowing where your leaders fall among these styles, it is equally important that you know your dominant or prevalent style in the workplace; this will allow you to better understand how or if your subordinates can approach you.

The talent management portion of the tool on the next page (must be used in conjunction with the strengths identification tool, under the "Duration" section, to be most effective) should be used to identify timing for movement to the next level. Evaluating the employee's time in the job, performance ratings, and last promotion date, highlights whether there are substantial gaps in time. This information should be used as a guide for planning future steps.

Talent Management and Planning Tool

Talent Management								
Current Date	Employee Name	Current Job Grade	Job Function	Time in Current Role	Technical Objective(s)	Personal Objective(s)	Last Promotion (date)	Last Three Performance Review Ratings (annual)

DURATION

How long will your canine sit for you? Is it just for a few seconds, and then he or she pops up and returns to a previous behavior or has to be told to sit again? Experience has and will continue to be a key element in career advancement. Being able to successfully perform your craft for an extended period of time provides the practice and familiarity with the skill required for mastery. However, varied experiences will help accelerate the knowledge process. Learning multiple commands for canines or skills for humans decreases the time needed for advancement. It is this diverse set of experiences that brings credibility needed for leadership opportunities.

Knowing the things you do well will certainly help in career advancement. When you do not have years of experience, you can create a comparable effect by gaining diverse experiences in areas important to your management and by amplifying strengths rather than just focusing on correcting weaknesses. A similar effect can be applied to your teams by having them focus less on identifying development opportunities (speak of them in terms of opportunities), and focus more of their time looking for ways to apply their strengths to accelerate the learning process. Balance is key, but when in doubt, lean more toward leveraging strengths.

A personal SWOT analysis is also a useful tool, where Strengths, Weaknesses, Opportunities, and Threats are identified based on the individual's (as opposed to the organization's) attributes. Again, strengths and opportunities should be the focus of this activity. A clear goal must be identified as the basis of the creation and application of the personal SWOT analysis. An individual can have multiple SWOT analyses: one for each of his or her high priority goals/objectives.

Personal SWOT Analysis

SWOT Analysis Questions

Strengths **S**	Weaknesses **W**
Opportunities **O**	Threats **T**

- **S**trengths: How will you continue to strengthen this attribute?

- **W**eaknesses: How will you strengthen this area? What resources are needed?

- **O**pportunities: How will you get access to these opportunities? How will you use these resources to achieve your goals?

- **T**hreats: How will you avoid things harmful to achieving your goal?

Strengths Identification Tool

The Strengths Identification Tool below should be used as the second part of the Talent Management Planning Tool. Similar to the SWOT, this guide allows managers to identify strengths and also plan next steps from a skill-set perspective. The major difference is that the SWOT is more of an individual tool as compared to the Strengths Identification Tool, which is used by managers to evaluate the collective strengths among their teams.

With the Strengths Identification Tool, an analysis can be performed to identify gaps between strengths and development opportunities. This gap analysis assessment can be used to create a personalized development plan for each team member. After the Strengths Identification and Talent Management Tools are completed for each member of the team, they should be combined and used to find the collective strengths of the team, to drive even greater performance.

Although predominately a team evaluation tool, as a leader, you can also complete this for yourself. Again, if your manager does not use this style of performance administration, care must be taken to present this at the right time and in the appropriate manner.

Strengths Identification						
Desired Next Step/Interest (Employee Perspective)	Strengths	Experiences	Development Opportunities	Actual Planned Next Steps (w/timing)	Are Employee Skills & Interests Being Considered?	Are the Employee Desired and Actual Next Steps Consistent? If No, Why?

Key Points—Chapter 3

- Three critical Ds are required for skill mastery, optimal performance, and sustainable results. Good leaders and strong teams are able to perform when distractions, distance, duration, are introduced.
- Be able to deliver exceptional performance even

when distractions are present.

- Be able to perform basic and complex functions independently (distant from your management), and prepare your team to perform in your absence (when distant from you).

- Being able to successfully perform your craft for long durations provides the practice and familiarity with the skill required for mastery. This process can be accelerated by gaining varied experiences and focusing on strength mastery.

CHAPTER 4

NETWORKING AND SOCIAL SKILLS

Canine instinct is not only useful for corporate survival but for advancement as well. Individuals who rise to the top respond with this type of intuition in situations when technical knowledge alone is insufficient. In other words, just knowing the facts and having data are simply not enough.

Canine interaction depends largely on the number of positive encounters that the canines have had in the past. Well-socialized canines can defuse situations and avoid fights, whereas poorly socialized canines fail to read subtle signs and choose a less positive option. Humans are no different. Situations are viewed from the lens of past experience. Without full awareness of your social surroundings, you are likely to have an incorrect reading of a situation. Being aware of past experiences, especially those that have created sensitivities, is necessary to avoid the victim mentality or an overly aggressive response to an innocent remark. Also, having the empathy to recognize where others may be coming from helps to understand different points of view.

Socialization is the foundation of human interaction. One form of socialization that is mandatory for engagement at all levels of an organization is networking. Networking can be viewed as making connections with the intent to build relationships. As you build your network, you should think about what you need/want to get out of each interaction, as well as what you can give back to each relationship. Networking can be accomplished through simple tasks like inviting others to talk over lunch, following up on contacts that you have made, and joining online professional groups. When deciding whether to network or not, keep in mind that networks play a critical role in determining the way problems are solved and organizations are run, and in the degree to which individuals succeed in achieving their goals. You should put some time and thought into building your professional network and think strategically about how to align with people from different backgrounds and work experiences; your personal network should include people who have overcome personal challenges different from your own. Developing the right social skills for interaction, especially among the executive ranks, sets the stage for upward progress. Well-socialized canines have figured out how to fine-tune their behavior to increase their chances of being accepted by other canines. They do this by adjusting their behavior to mimic that of the pack. Well-socialized humans with large networks experience similar acceptance by their kind as well. Having a diverse network is beneficial, but it is equally important to align with others who can work toward a shared vision.

Canines also find ways to approach other unknown canines in a wide arc rather than in a direct, confrontational manner. For humans, this translates to customizing your approach to dealing with individuals and meeting them at their individual levels of need. Leaders may have a known style that works for them and has brought them to their current level of success. However, many of them have had to flex this style along the rise to alpha positions until their credibility was established.

Consider the management styles discussed in Chapter 3: autocratic, paternalistic, democratic, and laissez-faire. While coming up the ranks, many aspiring leaders have used a democratic style to build loyalty. Leaders may have to adopt the paternalistic style when they are working with a new or inexperienced team. The democratic style may also be adopted when complex decisions need to be made that require input from team members who are skilled specialists. If managers are aware that they have a highly professional or creative group of employees, they may become more laissez-faire in their approach since their engagement may be required on a less frequent basis. Once you understand the current dominant management style and motivation of the leader you are approaching, you can adjust your approach accordingly. Conversely, you have to be aware of the style you are exhibiting to determine how or if you will be approached.

Although canine communication is quite limited, messages can be sent and received through body language, which also occurs with humans. For canines, a tucked tail signifies fear. For humans, limited eye contact, downward sloping head movement, and weak handshakes are signs of low self-esteem. These seemingly innocent behaviors almost always hinder individuals from establishing strong networks and disqualify them from acquiring alpha positions.

Summary of Key Socialization and Networking Attributes

Social interactions

- Canine interaction depends largely on the number of positive encounters that they have had in the past.
- Being aware of past experiences, especially those that have created sensitivities, is necessary to avoid overly aggressive response to an innocent remark.

Networking

- One form of socialization that is mandatory for engagement at all levels of an organization is networking. Developing the right social skills for interaction, especially among the executive ranks, sets the stage for upward progress.

Diversity

- Appreciating diversity is critical, but aligning with others who can work toward a shared organizational vision is highly valuable.
- For humans, this translates to customizing your approach to dealing with individuals and meeting them at their individual level of need.

Flexibility

- Leaders may have a known style that works for them and has brought them to their current level of success. However, many of them have had to flex this style along the rise to alpha positions until their credibility was established.

Empathy for management style

- Having the empathy to recognize where others may be coming from helps to understand different points of view. Socialization is the foundation of human interaction.

Key Points—Chapter 4

- Canine instinct is a valuable survival strategy.
- We as humans are not so different from canines in our social and behavioral responses, in many cases.
- Through commonality and understanding, shared experiences can be leveraged for learning and leading.

CHAPTER 5

DEVELOPING YOUR INSTINCT

Continuous improvement is an absolute necessity for advancement. For exceptional leaders, it should be an obligation to the teams being led.

Do I have it? When will it kick in? When can I start using it? Who will be able to tell?

So, how do you know? As we have learned, having canine instinct is not as simple as possessing just one attribute. It is a compilation of traits, behaviors, response mechanisms, and approaches to problem solving. When the principles discussed in the guide are practiced, they become a natural, positive way in which you respond to challenging situations. It starts with understanding the behavior and techniques by studying alpha leaders. The next step entails figuring out when and how to apply the methods to develop your leadership skills and the skills of your team.

Canine instinct doesn't just happen. It is acquired through awareness, hard work, discipline, and compassion. There will not be a box on any application that asks if you have it. Others will not explicitly know about your skill, but they will notice your increase in performance and constructive mode of operation. Canine instinct is a part of a transformation necessary for advancing to the next level of leadership. It comes with a responsibility to provide guidance and direction to others and a commitment to have resolute accountability.

NOW WHAT?

There are many other interactions that are similar to both canine and human interactions. The behaviors discussed in the guide are considered to be essential for both inside and outside the workplace.

In summary, alpha spots are reserved for leaders who can establish credibility, demonstrate flexibility, show empathy, set boundaries and limitations, apply appropriate corrections, perform well even under duress, and provide incentives. Although there are individuals currently in the alpha ranks who may not demonstrate these characteristics, new managers looking to break into the game will need to know and understand them. These aspiring senior leaders also have three additional responsibilities (discussed in Chapter 2) to master in the corporate game. They must execute the critical advancement activities and demonstrate the proper corporate conduct, in addition to having exceptional performance.

TAKING RESPONSIBILITY

The role of this document was simply to present one approach to teaching individuals to become more proactive at taking charge of their future. Fair or not, individuals must learn how to take ownership for the career they desire. Proactively navigating the corporate world will allow participants to gain access to opportunities, and from there, they can display their talents.

Success is all about gaining access to opportunities and positioning to secure the initial chance. Without this chance, it will be difficult for individuals to reach their true potential, and without a focus on continuous improvement, it will be impossible for them to exceed their potential. Alpha position seekers must continue to use these concepts in the future, as they are faced with increasingly more challenging life and business situations.

In general, individuals don't want to be unfairly given opportunities but instead want the opportunity to compete on equitable footing. True leaders must take their share of responsibility for creating these equitable opportunities, work diligently to deliver beyond assigned expectations, and then own the final outcome.

MOTIVATING OTHERS

Just as most people regard canines as the model of loyal behavior, the canine's need for attention and rewards is also well understood. When humans interact with canine pets, they almost always reach for a treat. But how many individuals have a clear plan for rewards in the workplace? Rewards are not just a requirement of the leadership ranks but should be practiced among all levels. Don't have a budget as an individual contributor? Then, a simple "thank you" will suffice. For leaders, this is one of the most important actions that can be used to bring about increased morale in any environment, from a board to the workplace to a committee. Treats are used by some animal trainers to bring about positive results quickly, by associating something good (the treats) with the desired behavior (the performance). Incentive-based organizations have proven to bring about consistent, sustainable change. Showing gratitude and interest in your team's work is an enormous step in the direction of being an empowering leader.

Sharing the learning experience is also essential and mutually beneficial for both the mentor and the mentee. The mentee obviously gains knowledge, but the mentor grows from imparting his or her expertise as well. By sharing experiences and lessons learned, the development process is accelerated, and the likelihood that the mentee will make similar mistakes is substantially reduced. Leaders use their workplace know-how as a team learning and engagement tool. This exchange is one of the most important elements needed to create and foster a strong team.

Workplace motivation is also gained through positive interactions between the leader and the team. These interactions include strategic direction and constructive feedback on performance. Encouragement and frequent discussions on development establish loyalty. Also, teaching teams to look for business opportunities, and identifying the developmental opportunities that go along with certain problems, are additional positive ways to drive performance.

Managers also gain reputations for being exceptional leaders when there is consistency between their messages and their actions. This creates trust and a foundation for building stronger workplace relationships.

In addition to the motivation of each individual member, team development is a prerequisite for superior collective accomplishment. Leaders who continuously deliver world-class performance realize that it is due in large part to the contribution of their teams. These exceptional leaders inspire those around them to reach for greater heights of achievement.

REVISITING THE MODEL

In the beginning of this document, the model below was introduced as a tool to help leaders view themselves in two ways: (1) as someone's manager, using this as an opportunity to coach and (2) as a subordinate of his or her manager, using this relationship as an opportunity to learn. All of the techniques and strategies from this document must be applied and practiced on both sides. The idea is that engaged, equipped, and empowered leaders create engaged, equipped, and empowered teams.

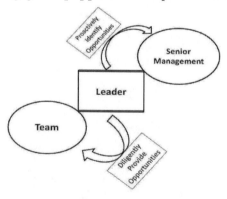

- The diagram below could be completed prior to learning the concepts from this document; however, now you should revisit your choices in light of the new information that you have acquired. In the diagram on the left (next page), for each box, you should be able to list activities and/or examples that have allowed you to make contributions (current state). In the diagram on the right (next page), you should list potential ways to advance your position (desired state). If there are gaps between the current and future state, a transitional plan or list of tasks and resources required to close the gap is necessary.

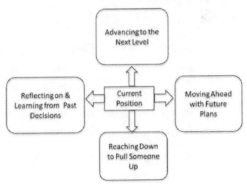

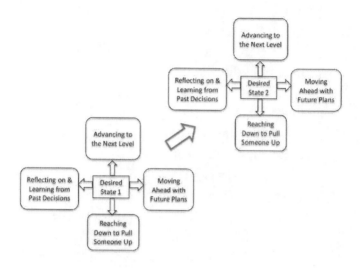

Key Points—Chapter 5

- Taking responsibility for making the necessary adjustments to style and content, sets apart outstanding leaders from mediocre ones.
- Proactively seeking counsel and refining your skills is the first step.
- Sharing what has been learned, for the benefit of others, is the honorable next step.

PARTING WORDS

This document is just one example of an innovative approach to solving a long-standing issue—how to obtain recognition and be rewarded with a position at the top of the heap. This information should be used along with continuous coaching from well-respected individuals within your network.

The techniques in the guide are not unique as individual learning points, but collectively, they represent a novel approach to career development. After reading this, those who continuously practice the techniques will be more likely to experience job progression. It is not a guarantee, but it is certainly an advantageous start in the right direction.

Knowing how to generate performance that establishes credibility is vital to securing any leadership position. Building a diverse network through positive interactions will strengthen your potential resource pool. Access to resources is a vital part of being equipped for the complex tasks that senior leaders face. Meeting others at their individual levels of need is best accomplished when you are willing to adapt your style and approach to meet the situation. Lastly, individuals who have sufficient compassion to view situations from the viewpoint of others will have yet another source to draw upon for additional tools, wisdom, and guidance. The goal is to use these techniques and tools to develop as an engaged, equipped, and empowered leader and to impart these same attributes to your team.

I continue to work tirelessly to share my experiences with others, through written material, lectures, training, etc. My motivation is simple: I truly believe that most people, if given a chance, will surprise the world by what they are capable of accomplishing.

I wish each of you success in fine tuning your instinct to advance to your desired level of achievement in the corporate world. Attainment is in reach.

REFERENCES

Management styles. (2009, February 2). In *Wikipedia, the free encyclopedia*. Retrieved February 8, 2009, from http://en.wikipedia.org/w/index.php?title=Management_styles&oldid=268119862.

Ammen, Amy. *Dog Training*. New York, NY: Howell Book House. 1998.

ABOUT THE AUTHOR

Dr. Ellen Burts-Cooper has been a successful manager in both the electronics manufacturing and the financial services industries.

Burts-Cooper is currently a vice president in the financial services industry. In her role, she is responsible for managing and delivering services for IT performance management. Burts-Cooper moved to Cleveland from St. Paul, Minnesota, in 2007 to serve as a Six Sigma Master Black Belt (MBB), leading a team of Lean and Six Sigma Black Belts to improve the quality and productivity of technology services provided to internal and external clients in the financial services industry.

Prior to the financial services industry, Burts-Cooper worked in the electronics industry, where she led global teams in several functions at a fortune 100 chemical manufacturing company in St. Paul, Minnesota, including research and development, new product commercialization, business/application development, and Six Sigma. She still consults and lectures in the area of new product development and works extensively with science outreach programs.

In addition to working in corporate America, Burts-Cooper is the founder and executive director of Improve Consulting and Training, a Minnesota-based firm that provides personal and professional development training, coaching, and consultation for youths and adults in transition. The model for Improve is to "empower individuals to exceed their potential." Burts-Cooper is the author of the workshop curricula "Personal Positioning: Building Personal Brand Equity" and "Don't Just Think Outside the Box, Make the Box Bigger." In addition to lecturing to both for-profit and nonprofit organizations, she also serves as an adjunct professor at Case Western in the Weatherhead School of Business MBA Program and guest lecturer at other colleges across the United States.

Burts-Cooper's passion is in the urban youth development area; however, she also actively volunteers and supports a host of community-related organizations across the United States.

Ellen attended Stillman College in Tuscaloosa, Alabama, where she received a BS in chemistry with a minor in mathematics. She earned a doctorate in organic/polymer chemistry from Virginia Tech in Blacksburg, Virginia. She completed her MBA at the University of Minnesota, Carlson School of Business.

As it relates to the credibility of writing this book, Ellen is also a certified canine trainer.

For more information on the seminars and workshops that accompany this document, visit www.improveconsultingbooks.com.

Research & Development

Dr. Burts-Cooper's unique approach to coaching helps individuals unleash their potential and yield results regardless of level or experience.
—A. Bowens-Jones, PhD, senior research scientist, Procter & Gamble, Cincinnati, Ohio

Academia

Ellen is a dynamic and inspirational life coach who leads and motivates by example!
—M. Simpson, PhD, director, Academic Program Review, Virginia Tech Graduate School, Blacksburg, Virginia
Dr. Burts-Cooper's style is engaging; her material is relevant and thought provoking.
—A. Green, PhD, assistant professor of science education, University of South Alabama, Mobile, Alabama

Retail

Ellen is very inspirational and has a unique approach to coaching and developing future leaders.
—D. Sally, district manager, Northeast Florida, Ross Clothing Stores, Jacksonville, Florida

Manufacturing

Ellen has the ability to very quickly analyze a person's strengths and development opportunities and create a plan to help that individual get the most out of his or her strengths and improve upon developmental opportunities.

—D. Isabelle, senior scientist, 3M Company, St. Paul, Minnesota

Banking

As a role model and mentor, Ellen has always encouraged me to work hard for the things that are important for my success. She stresses accountability and sacrifice, when needed, to get the job done.

—T. Foster, retail business owner and compliance specialist, Regions Bank, Birmingham, Alabama

Medical

Ellen is a driven and dedicated individual who is passionate about the education and motivation of her employees and colleagues.

—B. Sims, MD, PhD, neonatal/perinatal medicine, University of Alabama, Birmingham, Alabama